Pirate Ships Ahoy!

BY CINDY JENSON-ELLIOTT

Reading Consultant:
Barbara J. Fox
Reading Specialist
Professor Emerita
North Carolina State University

CAPSTONE PRESS
a capstone imprint

Blazers is published by Capstone Press,
1710 Roe Crest Drive, North Mankato, Minnesota 56003.
www.capstonepub.com

Library of Congress Cataloging-in-Publication Data
Jenson-Elliott, Cynthia L.
    Pirate ships ahoy! / by Cindy Jenson-Elliott.
    p. cm.—(Blazers. Pirates!)
    Includes bibliographical references and index.
    Summary: "Describes different types of pirate ships, how they were used, and how
pirates kept their ships in good shape"—Provided by publisher.
    Audience: Ages 6–12.
    ISBN 978-1-4296-8610-5 (library binding)
    ISBN 978-1-62065-203-9 (ebook PDF)
    1. Pirates—Juvenile literature. 2. Sailing ships—Juvenile literature. I. Title.
G535.J46 2013
910.4'5—dc23   2011048909

Editorial Credits
Aaron Sautter, editor; Veronica Correia, designer; Marcie Spence, media researcher;
    Laura Manthe, production specialist

Photo Credits
Alamy: Lebrecht Music and Arts Photo Library, 11, Print Collector, The, 15; Art Resource,
N.Y.: Alfredo Dagli Orit, 8-9, HIP, 26-27; Bridgeman Art Library: Calvados Art Ltd., 19,
Delaware Art Museum, Wilmington, 23, Giraudon, 5, Look and Learn, cover, Michael
Graham-Stewart, 7; Corbis: Bettmann, 25; Image Works, The: Fotomas/TopFoto, 13;
North Wind Picture Archives, 28; Shutterstock: Chantal de Bruijne, 16–17, Gordan, 20

Capstone Press would like to thank Alex Diaz at the St. Augustine Pirate and Treasure Museum
for his help in creating this book.

Printed in the United States of America in Stevens Point, Wisconsin.
032012   006678WZF12

Table of Contents

Ship Ahoy!

Large sails swell in the wind. The smell of salty water fills the air. The open ocean waits to be explored. Ships were a ticket to freedom for most pirates. On ships, pirates lived as they pleased.

Fact

Pirates usually stole merchant ships after taking them over. Pirates then changed the merchant ships into pirate ships.

Chapter One

Types of Pirate Ships

SCHOONERS

Most pirates liked small, fast ships. Schooners were thin and speedy. These ships had two **masts** to hold big sails. Pirates could hide schooners in shallow **coves** before making surprise attacks on merchant ships.

mast—a tall pole on a ship's deck that holds its sails

cove—a small, sheltered inlet or bay

SLOOPS AND BRIGANTINES

Sloops and brigantines had both sails and oars. Sloops had one mast with many sails. Brigantines had two masts with several square sails.

BRIGANTINE

Sometimes two or three small pirate ships worked as a team to attack a large merchant ship.

LARGE SHIPS

A few famous pirates used large warships with three masts. Large ships were heavy. They could not move or turn fast. But they carried more guns, crew, and **loot**.

loot—treasure taken from a ship or town

Black Bart's ship *Royal Fortune* was one of the largest ships ever sailed by a pirate. It carried 52 guns.

Chapter Two

Touring a Ship

THE DECK

Pirates worked on the ship's deck. Tall masts, a **boom**, and **rigging** held up the sails. Pirates often "cleared the deck" after stealing a ship. They replaced raised platforms with flat cannon decks.

boom—a long, horizontal pole that holds the bottom of a sail

rigging—the ropes on a ship that support and control the sails

There were two kinds of rigging on a ship. Standing rigging supported the mast. Running rigging pulled the sails up and down.

LIVING QUARTERS

Pirate crews slept in **hammocks** below deck. If there weren't enough hammocks, some pirates slept on deck. Some pirate captains had private cabins. But they often shared their cabins with the **quartermaster**.

hammock—a hanging bed made of canvas that is tied between two posts

quartermaster—a ship's officer who was in charge of the crew and divided treasure according to the rules

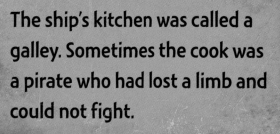

Fact

The ship's kitchen was called a galley. Sometimes the cook was a pirate who had lost a limb and could not fight.

THE HOLD

Supplies were stored in the **hold**. The hold was often located below the living quarters. Weapons, food, and loot were stored in the hold.

Fact

Pirates sometimes built secret rooms in the hold to hide their loot.

hold—the cargo space inside of a ship

Chases, Battles, and Escapes

Pirates needed fast ships to catch merchant ships and escape from enemies. Pirates often made changes after capturing a ship. They changed the ship's structure and rigging to make it lighter and faster.

Fact

During storms pirates "battened down the hatches." They closed doors to the ship's hold to keep water out.

19

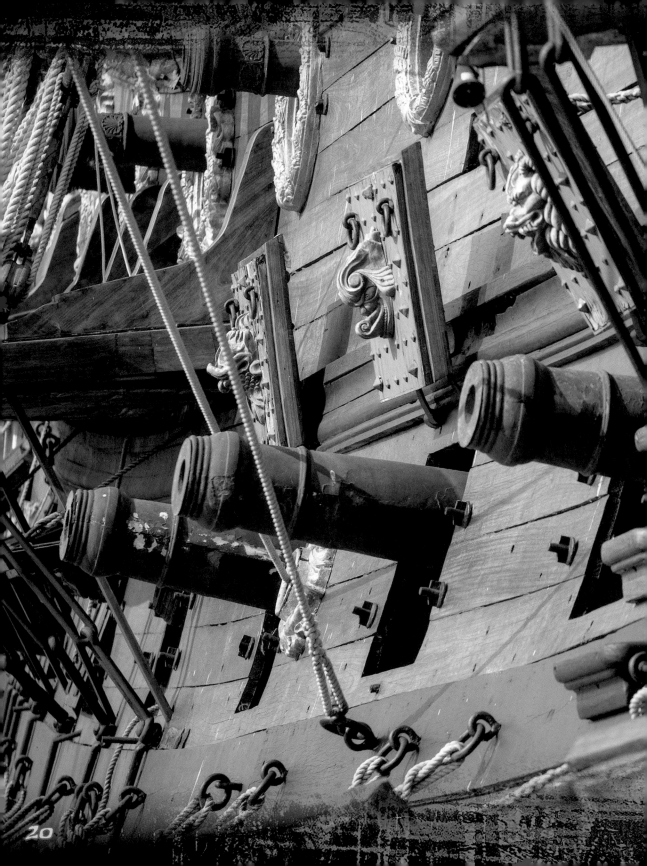

BATTLES

Pirate ships were built for battle. Cannons lined the deck or poked out of gun ports. Pirates usually fired a warning shot at merchant ships. They wanted to scare the merchant crew into giving up without a fight.

Fact

Firing "broadside" meant to turn the ship sideways toward an enemy ship. Every cannon would be fired at the same time to cause a lot of damage.

BOARDING PARTIES

Pirates boarded ships in raids. They first steered their ships next to a merchant ship. They used **boarding hooks** to pull the ships together. Then they climbed onto the other ship to fight with pistols and swords.

boarding hook—a metal hook used to grab onto the side of a ship

Fact

Sometimes pirates rowed a small boat next to a merchant ship. They would quietly climb in to surprise their victims.

Chapter Four

Ship Shape

Pirates kept their ships ready to chase victims and escape enemies. They worked hard to keep their ships in good shape. They made constant repairs to rigging, anchors, and sails.

Fact

Pirates mopped the ship's deck often to keep it clean.

REPAIRS AFTER BATTLE

Battles were hard on a ship. Pirates covered holes from enemy cannonballs with sheets of lead. Seams and small holes were filled with **oakum** and **pitch** to keep water out.

A broken mast meant the ship could not sail well. Pirates replaced broken masts as quickly as possible.

oakum—loose rope fibers mixed with tar

pitch—thick, sticky tar used for patching holes in a ship's hull

Pirates were in danger when their ship was careened. They could easily be caught.

CAREENING
THE SHIP

Pirates careened their ship every three to six months. They turned the ship on its side to clean off **barnacles**, worms, and snails. Pirates relied on their ships. They worked hard to keep their ships ready for action.

barnacle—a small shellfish that attaches itself to the sides of ships

barnacle (BAR-ni-kuhl)—a small shellfish that attaches itself to the sides and bottoms of ships

boarding hook (BORD-ing HOOK)—a metal hook used to grab onto the side of a ship and climb aboard

boom (BOOM)—a long, horizontal pole that holds the bottom of a sail

cove (KOHV)—a small, sheltered inlet or bay

hammock (HAM-uhk)—a hanging bed made of canvas that is tied between two posts

hold (HOHLD)—the cargo space inside of a ship

loot (LOOT)—treasure taken from a ship or town

mast (MAST)—a tall pole on a ship's deck that holds its sails

oakum (OH-kuhm)—loose rope fibers mixed with tar used for filling seams in a ship's hull

pitch (PICH)—thick, sticky tar used for patching holes in a ship's hull

quartermaster (KWOR-tur-mass-tur)—a ship's officer who was in charge of the crew and divided treasure according to the rules

rigging (RIHG-ing)—the ropes on a ship that support and control the sails

Read More

Havercroft, Elizabeth. *A Year On a Pirate Ship.* Time Goes By. Minneapolis: Millbrook Press, 2009.

Jenson-Elliott, Cindy. *Life Under the Pirate Code.* Pirates! Mankato, Minn.: Capstone Press, 2013.

Price, Sean. *Pirates: Truth and Rumors.* Truth and Rumors. Mankato, Minn.: Capstone Press, 2011.

Internet Sites

FactHound offers a safe, fun way to find Internet sites related to this book. All of the sites on FactHound have been researched by our staff.

Here's all you do:

Visit *www.facthound.com*

Type in this code: 9781429686105